BOOKWORMS

Go, Critter, Go!

Buzz, Bee, Buzz!

Dana Meachen Rau

Marshall Cavendish
Benchmark
New York

Bees are hairy.

Bees have six legs.

Bees have four wings.

Bees fly to flowers.

Bees go in hives.

Bees live with other bees.

Bees make wax.

Bees make honey.

Buzz, bee, buzz!

Words We Know

flower

hairy

hive

honey

legs

wax

wings

Index

About the Author

Dana Meachen Rau is an author, editor, and illustrator. A graduate of Trinity College in Hartford, Connecticut, she has written more than one hundred fifty books for children, including nonfiction, biographies, early readers, and historical fiction. She lives with her family in Burlington, Connecticut.

With thanks to the Reading Consultants:

Nanci Vargus, Ed.D., is an Assistant Professor of Elementary Education at the University of Indianapolis.

Beth Walker Gambro received her M.S. Ed. Reading from the University of St. Francis, Joliet, Illinois.

Marshall Cavendish Benchmark
99 White Plains Road
Tarrytown, New York 10591-9001
www.marshallcavendish.us

Library of Congress Cataloging-in-Publication Data

Rau, Dana Meachen, 1971–
Buzz, bee, buzz! / by Dana Meachen Rau.
p. cm. — (Bookworms. Go, critter, go!)
Summary: "Describes characteristics and behaviors of bees"—Provided by publisher.
Includes index.
ISBN-13: 978-0-7614-2648-6
1. Bees—Juvenile literature. I. Title. II. Series.
QL565.2.R38 2007
595.79'9—dc22
2006034227

Editor: Christina Gardeski
Publisher: Michelle Bisson
Designer: Virginia Pope
Art Director: Anahid Hamparian

Photo Research by Anne Burns Images

Cover Photo by Corbis/Bach/zefa

The photographs in this book are used with permission and through the courtesy of: Animals Animals: pp. 1, 7, 21B
Stehen Dalton; p. 13 Carson Baldwin, Jr.; p. 19 John Pontier. Corbis: pp. 3, 5, 15, 20TR, 21TL/TR Treat Davidson/Frank
Lane Picture Agency; pp. 9, 20TL Ralph A. Clevenger; pp. 11, 20BL Adam Woolfitt; pp. 17, 20BR Hans Reinhard/zefa.

Printed in Malaysia
1 3 5 6 4 2